THE EVOLUTION
OF AFRICA'S MAJOR NATIONS

Cameroon

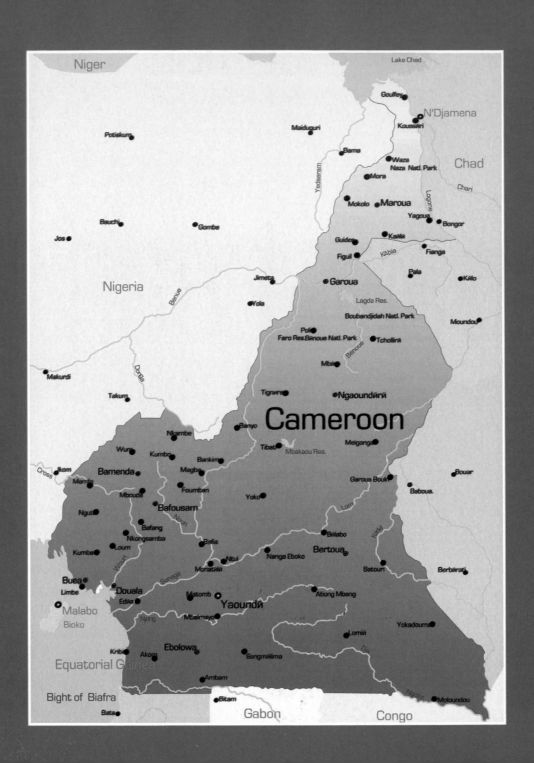

THE EVOLUTION
OF AFRICA'S MAJOR NATIONS

Cameroon

Diane Cook

Mason Crest
Philadelphia

Mason Crest
370 Reed Road
Broomall, PA 19008
www.masoncrest.com

CPSIA Compliance Information: Batch #EAMN2013-7. For further information,
contact Mason Crest at 1-866-MCP-Book.

First printing

1 3 5 7 9 8 6 4 2

Library of Congress Cataloging-in-Publication Data

Cook, Diane.
Cameroon / Diane Cook.
    p. cm. — (Evolution of Africa's major nations.)
Includes bibliographical references and index.
ISBN 978-1-4222-2194-5 (hardcover)
ISBN 978-1-4222-2222-5 (pbk.)
ISBN 978-1-4222-9434-5 (ebook)
1. Cameroon—Juvenile literature. I. Title. II. Series: Evolution of Africa's major nations.
DT564.C324 2012
967.11—dc22
                            2011018539

Table of Contents

Africa: Progress, Problems, and Promise

Robert I. Rotberg

Africa is the cradle of humankind, but for millennia it was off the familiar, beaten path of global commerce and discovery. Its many peoples therefore developed largely apart from the diffusion of modern knowledge and the spread of technological innovation until the 17th through 19th centuries. With the coming to Africa of the book, the wheel, the hoe, and the modern rifle and cannon, foreigners also brought the vastly destructive transatlantic slave trade, oppression, discrimination, and onerous colonial rule. Emerging from that crucible of European rule, Africans created nationalistic movements and then claimed their numerous national independences in the 1960s. The result is the world's largest continental assembly of new countries.

There are 53 members of the African Union, a regional political grouping, and 48 of those nations lie south of the Sahara. Fifteen of them, including mighty Ethiopia, are landlocked, making international trade and economic growth that much more arduous and expensive. Access to navigable rivers is limited, natural harbors are few, soils are poor and thin, several countries largely consist of miles and miles of sand, and tropical diseases have sapped the strength and productivity of innumerable millions. Being landlocked, having few resources (although countries along Africa's west coast have tapped into deep offshore petroleum and gas reservoirs), and being beset by malaria, tuberculosis, schistosomiasis, AIDS, and many other maladies has kept much of Africa poor for centuries.

Thirty-two of the world's poorest 44 countries are African. Hunger is common. So is rapid deforestation and desertification. Unemployment rates are often over 50 percent, for jobs are few—even in agriculture. Where Africa once was a land of small villages and a few large cities, with almost everyone engaged in growing grain or root crops or grazing cattle, camels, sheep, and goats, today more than half of all the more than 1 billion Africans, especially those who live south of the Sahara, reside in towns and cities. Traditional agriculture hardly pays, and a number of countries in Africa—particularly the smaller and more fragile ones—can no longer feed themselves.

There is not one Africa, for the continent is full of contradictions and variety. Of the 750 million people living south of the Sahara, at least 150 million live in Nigeria, 85 million in Ethiopia, 68 million in the Democratic Republic of the Congo, and 49 million in South Africa. By contrast, tiny Djibouti and Equatorial Guinea have fewer than 1 million people each, and prosperous Botswana and Namibia each are under 2.2 million in population. Within some countries, even medium-sized ones like Zambia (12 million), there are a plethora of distinct ethnic groups speaking separate languages. Zambia, typical with its multitude of competing entities, has 70 such peoples, roughly broken down into four language and cultural zones. Three of those languages jostle with English for primacy.

Given the kaleidoscopic quality of African culture and deep-grained poverty, it is no wonder that Africa has developed economically and politically less rapidly than other regions. Since independence from colonial rule, weak governance has also plagued Africa and contributed significantly to the widespread

The West African tribes that live in Cameroon wear carved masks like this one during traditional rituals and celebrations.

A village in rural Cameroon. In 2011, about 42 percent of Cameroon's population lived in rural areas.

poverty of its peoples. Only Botswana and offshore Mauritius have been governed democratically without interruption since independence. Both are among Africa's wealthiest countries, too, thanks to the steady application of good governance.

Aside from those two nations, and South Africa, Africa has been a continent of coups since 1960, with massive and oil-rich Nigeria suffering incessant periods of harsh, corrupt, autocratic military rule. Nearly every other country on or around the continent, small and large, has been plagued by similar bouts of instability and dictatorial rule. In the 1970s and 1980s Idi Amin ruled Uganda capriciously and Jean-Bedel Bokassa proclaimed himself emperor of the

Central African Republic. Macias Nguema of Equatorial Guinea was another in that same mold. More recently Daniel arap Moi held Kenya in thrall and Robert Mugabe has imposed himself on once-prosperous Zimbabwe. In both of those cases, as in the case of Gnassingbe Eyadema in Togo and the late Mobutu Sese Seko in Congo, these presidents stole wildly and drove entire peoples and their nations into penury. Corruption is common in Africa, and so are a weak rule-of-law framework, misplaced development, high expenditures on soldiers and low expenditures on health and education, and a widespread (but not universal) refusal on the part of leaders to work well for their followers and citizens.

Conflict between groups within countries has also been common in Africa. More than 12 million Africans have been killed in civil wars since 1990, while another 9 million have become refugees. Decades of conflict in Sudan led to a January 2011 referendum in which the people of southern Sudan voted overwhelmingly to secede and form a new state. In early 2011, anti-government protests spread throughout North Africa, ultimately toppling long-standing regimes in Tunisia and Egypt. That same year, there were serious ongoing hostilities within Chad, Ivory Coast, Libya, the Niger Delta region of Nigeria, and Somalia.

Despite such dangers, despotism, and decay, Africa is improving. Botswana and Mauritius, now joined by South Africa, Senegal, Kenya, and Ghana, are beacons of democratic growth and enlightened rule. Uganda and Senegal are taking the lead in combating and reducing the spread of AIDS, and others are following. There are serious signs of the kinds of progressive economic policy changes that might lead to prosperity for more of Africa's peoples. The trajectory in Africa is positive.

Many types of terrain can be found in the West African country known as Cameroon. (Opposite) A high waterfall in the tropical jungle. (Right) Low hills on the savanna, or grasslands, near Ngaoundal in Cameroon's Adamawa Province. The Adamawa Plateau of central Cameroon has an average elevation of 3,300 feet (1,000 meters).

Africa in One Country

IF ANY NATION could represent the great diversity that is Africa, it is Cameroon. The country's landscape captures the beauty and mystique of the continent: rainforests, beaches, lava beds, thermal springs, *terraced* hillsides, rustic villages, and exotic plants and animals. In short, Cameroon has a little bit of everything that is Africa inside its 183,568 square miles (475,440 square kilometers).

Slightly larger than the state of California, Cameroon, located in West Africa, is bordered on the southwest by the Atlantic Ocean and on the north by the Sahara Desert. It is surrounded by six countries: Nigeria, Chad, the Central African Republic, the Republic of Congo, Gabon, and Equatorial Guinea.

Cameroon has ten major rivers, which feed into four large water systems across the country. In the south, the Ntem, Wouri, Nyong, and Sanaga rivers

THE GEOGRAPHY OF CAMEROON

Location: Western Africa, bordering the Bight of Biafra, between Equatorial Guinea and Nigeria

Area: (slightly larger than California)
  total: 183,568 square miles (475,440 square km)
  land: 182,514 square miles (472,710 square km)
  water: 2,730 square miles (7,071 square km)

Borders: Central African Republic, 495 miles(797 km); Chad, 680 miles (1,094 km); Republic of the Congo, 325 miles (523 km); Equatorial Guinea, 118 miles (189 km); Gabon, 185 miles (298 km); Nigeria, 1,050 miles (1,690 km)

Climate: varies with terrain, from tropical along coast to semiarid and hot in north

Terrain: diverse, with coastal plain in southwest, dissected plateau in center, mountains in west, plains in north

Elevation extremes:
  lowest point: Atlantic Ocean, 0 feet (0 m)
  highest point: Fako (on Mount Cameroon) 13,435 feet (4,095 m)

Natural hazards: volcanic activity with periodic releases of poisonous gases from Lake Nyos and Lake Monoun volcanoes

Source: CIA World Factbook, 2011.

empty into the Atlantic. The Bénoué and Kébi rivers in the north become part of the Niger River basin. Further north, the Logone and Chari rivers empty into Lake Chad, while the Ngoko River joins the Sangha, which flows into the Congo River.

SOUTHERN GEOGRAPHICAL REGION

Cameroon's southern geographical region covers an area that runs 226 miles (364 km) from the Atlantic coastline east to the Middle Congo Basin between Cameroon's southern frontier and the Sanaga River.

Much of the south is dominated by a rainforest-covered *plateau* that rises 960 feet (293 meters) above sea level. This region extends eastward towards the Central African Republic. The plateau's climate includes a dry season from November to February, light rains from March to May, and heavy rains from June to October. The most humid season is in July and August.

Along the Atlantic coast, the climate is hot and humid because of its location near the equator. The southwest region around the town of Debundscha, near the coastal town of Limbe, is one of the wettest regions in the world. For cities like Douala—a major port in the Littoral Province—the rainy season presents a significant challenge. In July and August, when the average monthly rainfall is over 15 inches (39 centimeters), hazardous flooding is common. The flooding often forces people to leave their homes and interrupts commerce and communications.

The country's generous rainfall is beneficial to the south's low coastal plains and the thick, equatorial rainforest that thrives all the way to the Sanaga River into Central Cameroon. This rainforest is humid and tropical and it enjoys two rainy seasons: September to November and April to May. Its drier seasons are from December to March and June to August. The average annual temperature is 77° Fahrenheit (25° Celsius), and the annual rainfall ranges from 67.8 inches (172 cm) to 90 inches (228.6 cm).

PLANTS AND ANIMALS OF MOUNT CAMEROON

Not far from Douala is one of the country's largest volcanoes, Mount Cameroon. It has a recorded eruption history dating back to the fifth century B.C. It also erupted in 1900, 1922, 1959, 1982, 1999, and 2000. At 13,436 feet

(4,095 m) tall, Mount Cameroon is the highest mountain in West Africa. It is also the only mountain close to the Atlantic Coast.

Mount Cameroon supports roughly 370,658 acres (150,000 hectares) of lowland and mountainous tropical forest. A biologically diverse region, many of its *indigenous* plants and animals are considered endangered species.

At least 42 plant species are unique to the Mount Cameroon area, like the *Prunus Africana*. Traditional healers use its bark to reduce fever and cure chest infections. Healers use the *Catharanthus roseus*, or Madagascar periwinkle, to treat leukemia and other blood cancers, while juice extracted from its leaves is used to treat diabetes, diarrhea, and toothaches.

More than 370 types of birds live on Mount Cameron, including two unique species. The Mount Cameroon Francolin has a red bill and red legs. It is usually found on the southeast slopes of the mountain, and can be identified by its high-pitched song, which sounds like a triple whistle. The Mount Cameroon speirops is a small, warbler-like bird with a noticeable white throat, forehead, and narrow white eye-ring. Other exotic birds that live in the region include the Grey-necked Picathartes, a bald, non-migratory bird; the Shining Drongo, a perching bird that aggressively protects its nest; and the Blue-breasted Kingfisher, a large kingfisher that reaches 9.5 inches tall.

In addition to exotic birds, several fascinating mammals live around Mount Cameroon. These include the Preuss's monkey, which has dark fur and a white chin; the drill, a short-tailed olive-colored forest baboon; and the Red-eared monkey, a quiet animal with a distinctive red tail, a red spot on its nose, and red-tipped ears. Unfortunately, all three are on the endangered

The western lowland gorilla is one of many animial species that live in Cameroon. These elusive apes inhabit some of Africa's densest and most remote rainforests.

species list. Larger animals like the forest elephant, the chimpanzee, and the western bush pig are a few of the many species that have made Mount Cameroon their home, along with smaller varieties like lizards and chameleons.

Unfortunately, urbanization around Mount Cameroon is crowding indigenous wildlife out of their habitat. For instance, about 300,000 of the people living around Mount Cameroon survive by harvesting forest timber. They cut down the trees, forcing animals out of their homes and eliminating their food supply. The expansion of farmland also leaves less land for animals to live in, making their survival more difficult.

LOGGING OF THE RAINFOREST

Mount Cameroon is not the only area affected by logging. The southern high plains—the habitat for many huge trees like acajou mahogany, limba, and azobe—are also being harvested for lumber. About 76 percent, or more than

42 million acres (17 million hectares), of Cameroon's 56.3 million acres (22.8 million hectares) of forests have either been logged or are allocated as logging concessions. Less than a fifth of the country's unprotected forests (mostly in central and eastern Cameroon) remain free from logging. Cameroon lost 18 percent of its forest cover, or 10.9 million acres (4.4 million hectares), between 1990 and 2010.

Cameroon's forests serve as home for chimpanzees, a rare antelope called the bongo, elephants, and leopards. Lowland gorillas still live in the wild in Cameroon, making the country one of the last habitats for this species. Around 5,000 western lowland gorillas live in the Lobeke National Park in southern Cameroon.

CENTRAL GEOGRAPHICAL REGION

Central Cameroon forms a natural barrier between the north and south. On the northern side of the Sanaga River, the forest fades into a sparse plain, which contains a scattering of trees and shrubs among the beautiful grasses. This vista extends to the Adamawa (also spelled Adamaoua) mountain range.

The central region, called the Adamawa Plateau, stretches from the western highlands to the eastern border and from the Sanaga River to the Bénoué River. From south to north the elevation climbs from 2,450 feet (747 m) to 4,450 feet (1,356 m). North of the Bénoué River, the land drops as it nears the Lake Chad basin. Scattered around the plains are mounds of erosion-resistant rock called inselbergs.

The average annual rainfall for the central region is about 60 inches (152 cm). There are four seasons, delineated by their precipitation: a dry season from December to May, a light rain from May to June, a dry season from July to October, and heavy rain from October to November.

Throughout the *savanna*, forest areas alternate with cultivated land. Domesticated livestock like goats, sheep, pigs, and cattle now occupy habitats where wild animals once freely roamed.

NORTHERN GEOGRAPHICAL REGION

Stretching northward from the foot of the plateau to Lake Chad are the great northern plains, where savannas contrast with the Mandara Mountains. The highest peak of the Mandara Mountains reaches 4,593 feet (1,400 m); lower areas are extensively terraced with small farms.

The north does not receive as much rain as the southern region. Average rainfall is 40 inches (102 cm), though this total varies greatly depending on how far north the land is. The dry season starts in November and lasts through March. The temperature in the northern town of Kousseri can hit 104°F (40°C) during the day from March to May.

Wild herds of rhinoceros, buffalo, elephant, and harnessed guib (an antelope with white markings that look like a harness) tend to roam the region's four national parks. Lions, giraffes, hyenas, leopards, Nile crocodiles, black and white colobus, mantled guereza, red-fronted gazelles, sun squirrels, baboons, and warthogs are can also be found in the region.

(Opposite) A Cameroonian soldier prepares to hoist his country's flag over the Bakassi Peninsula. In August 2006 Nigeria turned over control of the disputed, oil-rich territory to Cameroon. (Right) Cameroon's first president, Ahmadou Ahidjo, shakes hands with military personnel and State Department officials during a 1982 visit to the United States.

2 A Cross-Cultural History

THE RECORD OF WEST AFRICA'S PAST comes to historians through oral tales blended with written histories. From these sources it is clear that many nations converged at the crossroads now called Cameroon. While invasions and migration from surrounding lands ushered in new cultures, the changes over the centuries were gradual. When the Europeans arrived in Africa, however, change accelerated, creating the modern state of Cameroon.

PEOPLE OF THE SOUTH

Among the first known people to live in what is now called Cameroon were the Pygmy Baka. Historians believe the Baka arrived around 10,000 years ago, but they are uncertain of the tribe's origin. The Baka settled in the vibrant rainforests of southern and eastern Cameroon. They are identified as pygmies because of their height, which is generally less than five feet (1.524 m). They speak the Baka language and continue to be *nomadic* hunter-gatherers who revere the spirit of the rainforest.

When Bantu-speaking farmers migrated into Cameroon about 2,200 years ago, they established trade relations with the Baka. Some historians believe the Bantu came from the Bénoué-Cross rivers area in southeastern Nigeria. Their gradual move south might have been a response to the drying of the Sahara Desert and a need to find *fertile* lands.

PEOPLE OF THE NORTH

While the Bantu-speaking people were settling into the south and the east, Arabic speakers from North Africa were settling in the northern region of present-day Cameroon. In the extreme north—near the town of Kousseri and Lake Chad—the Sao were the earliest-known inhabitants. They were eventually conquered and absorbed by the raiding Kanem-Borno around the eighth or ninth century.

The Kanem-Borno Empire was a *federation* of nomadic tribes that migrated into northern Cameroon from Chad. They ruled the region as part of their empire for about a thousand years. Eventually, however, the Kanem-Borno Empire grew weaker and began to lose control of the area. Their decline was hastened by the arrival of the Fulani. These nomadic herdsmen migrated from Senegal into the region between the 13th and 15th centuries, looking for better grazing land for their cattle. Pleased with the Chadian basin, the Fulani started building settlements.

Many of the Fulani were Muslims, or followers of a religion called Islam. Muslims believe that Allah is the only god and that Muhammad, an Arab who lived between A.D. 570 and 632, was a prophet who brought Allah's teachings to mankind. Muslims consider their religion a comprehensive system of life, and believe it is their duty to spread the religion to others. In the early 19th century, Fulani Muslims in Nigeria mounted a *jihad*, or holy war, against the Hausa people, conquering several communities and converting many of the villagers. As the *jihad* spread into northern Cameroon, some non-Fulani people escaped into the hills, while others accepted the Fulani conquest.

PEOPLE OF THE WEST

As Cameroon's population increased, several tribes that spoke a variation of the Bantu language—the Tikar, the Bamoun, and the Bamileke—established themselves in the western part of the country.

The Tikar encompassed multiple ethnic groups who came from Nigeria. They settled around the towns of Tibati, Banyo, Kimi, Ndobo, and Ngaoundéré. About 300 years ago, internal dissension combined with a desire for new land split the tribes. Some tribes came under the leadership of a Tikar ruler's sons, and these leaders called themselves *fon* (which means paramount chief or king). These Tikar migrated south and west to what is now the city of Bamenda.

While the Bamouns date back to the 14th century, it was Prince Nshare Yen who fully established their tribe in the 16th century. During the next 300 years, the Bamouns absorbed neighboring villages. By the 19th century,

Sultan Ibrahim Njoya (ca. 1876–1933) was an influential ruler of the Bamoun people.

under the leadership of Sultan Ibrahim Njoya, the Bamouns became a powerful, centralized state. Njoya reigned for more than 49 years. His accomplishments included developing a system of writing for his language; establishing schools throughout his kingdom so his people could learn to read and write; and compiling a history of the kingdom and a book of court laws.

The final dominant group in western Cameroon, the Bamileke, are a collection of ethnic groups who live mostly in the nation's western highlands. Though no one can say for certain why they left the Adamawa Plateau, the Bamileke crossed the upper Mbam River and moved south in a succession of five waves. Splitting into small groups, these new tribes then built new villages, or *fons*. As various Bamileke *fons* emerged in the region, more civil wars erupted.

EUROPEAN INVASION

In 1472 a Portuguese businessman hired a sailor named Fernando Po to explore the African coast and find a trade route to Asia. During his journey Po became the first European to explore the interior of what today is Cameroon. He sailed his ship up an **estuary**, which he named Rio dos Camaroes (meaning

"River of Prawns"). The country later took its name from the river, although the estuary's name was eventually changed to the Wouri River.

Po and his fellow explorers started providing European products to local chieftains in exchange for various *commodities*, including gold, ivory, and slaves that the chiefs' armies had captured during tribal skirmishes.

There was a great demand for slaves during the 16th and 17th centuries, as European countries like Spain, Portugal, the Netherlands, England, and France began to establish colonies in North America, South America, and the Caribbean. To exploit the resources of these lands, the Europeans needed an inexpensive source of labor. Slaves from Africa could be used to mine for gold or silver, or to care for profitable crops like sugar cane, tobacco, and rice on large plantations. As a result, the slave trade was very profitable both for the African chiefs and for the European slavers. Experts estimate that over a 400-year period, more than 10 million Africans were uprooted from their homes and shipped across the Atlantic to work as slaves.

Gradually, European attitudes toward slavery changed. In 1807 the government of Great Britain declared that the transatlantic slave trade was illegal. It sent its powerful navy to patrol the Atlantic Ocean off the coast of West Africa to enforce this ban. But the British could not stop every ship. The slave trade continued secretly in the Cameroon area until some traders from Douala determined that selling ivory and palm oil was safer and more profitable. Douala eventually became the most important trading center on the Cameroon River.

At the time that the slave market was declining, northern Cameroon was an empire of emirates centrally controlled by the Fulani in Sokoto (Nigeria).

In the south local tribes were free from outside control, and often traded with German, French, and British merchants. However, this period of rule by Africans was about to end.

EUROPEAN COLONIZATION

Before the 19th century, few Europeans ventured into the unfriendly African interior. Wild animals, diseases like malaria, and thick forests kept would-be settlers and missionaries from venturing too far inland. But by the mid-1800s Europeans were more willing to explore Africa and establish colonies.

In 1842 the English Baptist Missionary Society established a small worship center on the island of Bioko. Two years later a Baptist church and school were established at Bimbia, a Spanish trading post on the Cameroon River. However, in 1845 the British navy abandoned their base on Bioko, and in 1858 the Spanish forced the Baptists to leave Bimbia.

Alfred Saker, who had joined the Baptists in 1843, refused to leave Cameroon. Instead, Saker bought land from a local chieftain, King William of Bimbia, and founded Victoria, a permanent settlement at the foot of Mount Cameroon.

The 1880s were a period of increased European activity in Africa, as countries like France, Germany, England, and Portugal claimed territories in order to control their resources. Although some local chieftains in the Cameroon region offered to sign treaties with the British in exchange for protection, the British government was not interested. It was more concerned about its valuable colonies in south and east Africa. Germany, however, was interested in *annexing* Cameroon. Like other European countries, Germany was looking for raw materials to import and new markets for its exports. The Germans decided they needed to establish permanent settlements to secure a competitive advantage. After signing agreements with several local chieftains along the Cameroon River in July 1884, German Commissioner Gustav Nachtigal started a colony called Kamerun on the Gulf of Biafra.

Competition with other European countries over land claims forced the Germans to venture deeper inland to protect their trading interests and to ensure a more reliable supply of raw materials. Settlers soon explored the interior of Cameroon and extended the land claimed by Germany to Lake Chad. (German Kamerun was larger than the present state of Cameroon, and included some territory now part of Nigeria.) Once Germany's political authority was established in the area, other European nations recognized Germany's claim to Kamerun.

But colonization was not easy. In 1885 the first governor, Julius Freiherr von Soden, had to focus his resources on crushing rebellions by the Bafut, Bulu, and Kpe tribes in the interior. After a decade of fighting and poor trade results, von Soden was replaced by Jesko Albert Eugen von Puttkamer. He was more effective at supressing the rebels, and used forced labor to build Cameroon's first railroad.

The German administrator Gustav Nachtigal started the Kamerun colony, and eventually brought the entire region under German control.

The German government did not want to spend a lot of money modernizing and developing

Cameroon's economy, so colonial authorities decided to follow the example set by other European nations. In 1899 they gave *monopoly* rights to two German companies: the Gesellschaft Sud-Kamerun and Gesellschaft Nordwest Kamerun. This gave these two corporations the opportunity to exploit and develop the land's resources and to establish law enforcement mechanisms to protect their profits.

On June 15, 1896, the German government declared all unoccupied land in Cameroon to be government property. This made it practically impossible for anyone but the trading companies to acquire land. Although the Germans promised to protect indigenous groups, in reality they were forced onto reservations too small to support them.

Colonial troops stand at attention outside a German government office in Ebolowa, Kamerun, circa 1890. Under German rule roads and bridges were built throughout the territory.

To make their plantation-based society work, land managers needed laborers to perform hundreds of jobs to support the estates: domestic activities in the planters' homes; planting and harvesting; carrying products from the trading stations into the interior; and building the roads and railroads. About 80,000 African porters were employed to carry goods for the Europeans on the 120-mile (193 km) trade route between Yaoundé and Kribi. But the amount they were paid would barely support one person, much less a family.

The exploitive conditions made the Cameroonian people uncooperative and most continued to work for themselves rather than the Germans, creating a significant labor shortage. To address this, the government imposed a head tax in the city of Douala on July 1, 1903.Each adult man and unmarried woman had to pay a tax of three marks per year. Married men with more than one wife were required to pay two marks for each additional wife. Even if they didn't have a job that paid money, the people had to pay the tax.

The strategy worked so well in Douala that on October 20, 1908, the German governors doubled the tax and expanded it to include all the people of Cameroon. In 1913 the tax was raised to 10 marks. People who could not pay the tax were forced to work on public service projects for 30 days. By 1914 this tax had achieved its objective—because many people could not afford to pay, they had no alternative but to work for the government. The tax generated government income of 2.8 million marks in revenue and an estimated 150,000 marks in free labor every year.

Though the Germans were harsh taskmasters, colonial rule transformed Cameroon from a *feudal* society to an *exchange economy*. One of the Germans' most significant contributions during this period was the development of the *infrastructure* necessary for the country's growth. By 1914 Cameroon had harbors in Douala, Kribi, Camp, and Tiko-Victoria. The colony had more than 250 miles (402 km) of railroad tracks, and laborers working for the government had built bridges, roads, paths, and impressive buildings, both public and private. The transition to a functional European exchange economy took less than 20 years.

CHANGING OF THE GUARD

In August 1914 war broke out in Europe when Germany invaded Belgium. The war soon developed into a worldwide conflict that pitted the Allied powers—France, Russia, Great Britain, Italy, and, after 1917, the United States—against the Central Powers—Germany, Austria-Hungary, the Ottoman Empire, and Bulgaria. Although much of the fighting took place in Europe, where years of brutal trench warfare left millions dead, military campaigns were waged throughout the world. In 1916, Belgian, French, and British soldiers captured Kamerun.

After World War I ended in November 1918, the victorious Allied powers stripped the defeated Central Powers of their colonies and redistributed them amongst themselves. In 1922 the League of Nations, an international organization established after the 1919 Paris Peace Conference and dedicated to preventing future wars through negotiation and diplomacy, divided Cameroon between two countries. France received a *mandate* to control 80 percent of the territory, while Britain received the remainder.

The French, who ruled from Yaoundé, educated a group of Cameroonians in French language, culture, and administrative procedures.

These elites served as colonial officers in the villages of French Cameroon and had considerable political and economic power. Like the Germans, the French used forced labor to build more railroads and other construction projects. The British, whose territory included a strip bordering Nigeria from the sea to Lake Chad, governed from Lagos, Nigeria. They took a different approach to administration, allowing local leaders to rule their villages or territories, and collect taxes that would be paid to the British government.

Ultimately, natives of Cameroon resented European domination. They wanted to govern themselves, and hoped for a restructured system that would give all residents greater social and economic benefits. Both the British and the French heard the cries for a change of the status quo, particularly after the end of World War II in 1945. After the war the United Nations, a new international organization of states, replaced the League of Nations. Cameroon and other former mandates became U.N. Trust Territories, which were supposed to be prepared for independence as quickly as possible. However, in most cases this took more than a decade, and many Africans felt that the European powers were not moving fast enough to turn over control.

MOVEMENT TOWARD INDEPENDENCE

In both British Cameroon and French Cameroon, protests and demands for independence continued throughout the 1950s. One important party in French Cameroon was the Union of the Peoples of Cameroon (UPC), which consisted of Bamileke, Bassa, and French-educated Fulani groups. In 1955 the UPC started violent riots for independence in French Cameroon. Thousands died during the rebellion, and damage to property was great. In response, the French government outlawed the UPC, preventing it from participating in the political process. The UPC-fueled violence continued even after French Cameroon gained its independence. It is estimated that more than 10,000 Africans died in the unrest.

In 1960, the Republic of Cameroon was established as an independent state. A Fulani politician named Ahmadou Ahidjo was elected as the country's first president.

In neighboring British Cameroon, the people were divided on the issue of their territory's future. Most of the residents of northern British Cameroon were Muslims. They were interested in joining the neighboring state of Nigeria, which had become independent from British rule in October 1960, because it also had a large Muslim population. The people of southern British Cameroon, however, preferred to become part of the Republic of Cameroon. After a *plebiscite* confirming these sentiments was held in October 1961, the British territory was divided between Nigeria and the Republic of Cameroon.

EARLY YEARS OF THE NATION

As president from 1960 to 1982, Ahmadou Ahidjo took the new nation from a weak, export-dependent economy to a stable, self-sufficient country. Avoiding the temptation to accept foreign loans that would put his country into debt, Ahidjo diversified his economy and invested in health care, education, and infrastructure. He encouraged agriculture so the nation could feed itself, and during his presidency Cameroonian farmers began to export many new commodities, including cocoa and coffee.

But Ahidjo's leadership was not without problems. From 1961 to 1963, there were problems between the French-speaking and the English-speaking people of Cameroon. The outlawed UPC also continued fighting government forces well into the 1960s. With the help of French soldiers, Ahidjo maintained order in the country. To suppress threats to his authority, he censored the press, imprisoned political opponents, and outlawed all political parties but his own, the Cameroon People's Democratic Movement (CPDM).

In 1972 the nation received a new constitution and a new name: the United Republic of Cameroon. Despite the new name and new constitution, the English-speaking Cameroonians (known as Anglophones), who were a minority in the country, felt *marginalized* and oppressed by French-speakers (known as Francophones).

Ahmadou Ahidjo helped Cameroon gain independence, and served as president until 1982.

PASSING THE BATON

In November 1982 Ahidjo resigned as president and allowed Paul Biya, his prime minister, to succeed him. Biya promised to implement reforms and deal with government corruption, and at first he seemed to be moving toward a more democratic system. He allowed open elections for the country's legislature and repealed some of Ahidjo's repressive laws. However, a year after Biya took office, Ahidjo attempted to regain power through a *coup* against the government. When the coup failed, the former president was forced into exile in France. After this, Biya's administration became less democratic, and he maintained the one-party system that his predecessor had established in 1966.

In 1984, Cameroon came to the attention of international scientists who wished to study a strange and deadly phenomenon known as a *limnic eruption*. This occurs when a body of water becomes saturated with carbon dioxide and unexpectedly releases a large cloud of the gas. On August 15, 1984, a gas cloud at Lake Mounon, in western Cameroon, killed 37 people. Two years later, in August 1986, a deadlier limnic eruption occurred in northwestern Cameroon, at Lake Nyos. The huge gas cloud suffocated more than 1,500 people and 3,500 livestock.

CAMEROON TODAY

Biya won several elections for president during the 1980s. In March 1990, however, 35,000 people demonstrated for democracy in Bamenda; six people died and many were injured after the military tried to contain the demonstration. A wave of strikes and protests paralyzed the country until Biya promised government reforms. At the end of 1990, new laws were passed that permitted multiple political parties to participate in elections.

Despite this change to the political system, and additional changes that were promised (but never implemented) when the constitution was

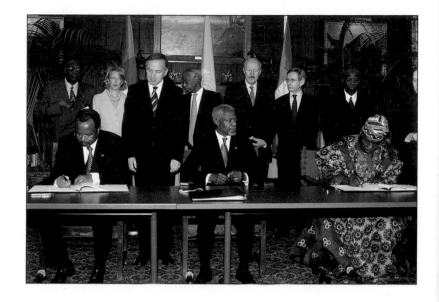

President Paul Biya of Cameroon (left) and President Olusegun Obasanjo of Nigeria (right), along with United Nations Secretary-General Kofi Annan (center) sign an agreement regarding the two countries' dispute on the Bakassi Peninsula. In August 2006 Nigeria turned over control of the disputed, oil-rich territory to Cameroon.

reformed in 1996, Biya and his cronies have maintained their hold on power. Opposition parties boycotted the 1997 election because of police crackdowns on those who opposed the Biya regime. Biya was re-elected president in 2004. In the fall of 2011, after another constitutional change eliminated limits on the number of terms the president can serve, Biya was elected again with almost 78 percent of the vote.

Today, Cameroon is politically stable but its underlying problems remain unresolved. The state is consistently ranked among the most corrupt countries in the world. In 2011 the government watchdog group Transparency International ranked Cameroon 134th out of 183 countries on its annual corruption index. Many other problems, including unpaid salaries in the public sector, social problems, poor health care and educational facilities, and economic issues continue to stir periodic unrest.

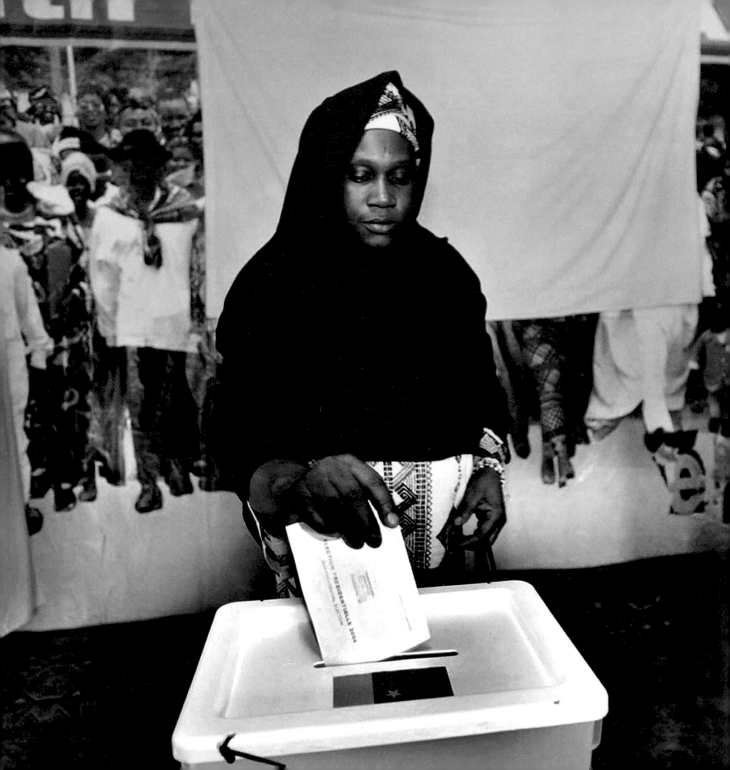

(Opposite) A Cameroonian woman casts her ballot at a polling station. Many international observers feel that Cameroon's elections are not fair, and that government intimidation and fraud are widespread. (Right) This building in Yaounde houses Cameroon's National Assembly, the country's legislative body.

3 Politics of Cameroon

CAMEROON HAS A STRONG CENTRAL GOVERNMENT, which is dominated by the president. Although the people of Cameroon do vote for their leaders, most experts do not consider the country a true democracy. Government leaders ensure they will stay in power by rigging elections, arresting political opponents, and intimidating voters.

On January 18, 1996, Cameroon adopted a new constitution, which was supposed to take some power away from the executive branch of government, redistributing it more evenly to the legislative and judicial branches. The constitution also permitted multiple political parties to form and compete in national and local elections. However, even today many of the constitution's reforms and provisions have not been implemented.

EXECUTIVE BRANCH

The most important government official in Cameroon is the president, who serves as the country's head of state. He is responsible for determining national policy; overseeing the operation of the state; ensuring that the country complies with international laws, treaties, and conventions; and enforcing the constitution and the laws.

Unlike in the United States and other countries, the president of Cameroon has a great deal of control over the other branches of government. The president can lengthen or shorten the term of the legislature, can veto laws that the legislature passes, and can appoint or dismiss judges. He also appoints and dismisses other government leaders, including the prime minister, cabinet members, generals, provincial governors, some local leaders, and heads of the nation's 100 state-controlled organizations.

According to the 1996 constitution, the president is elected for a seven-year term. Originally, the president could only be re-elected once, but the two-term limit was lifted by the National Assembly in 2008. The current president, Paul Biya, has held the post for more than a quarter-century. He became president on November 6, 1982, when Ahmadou Ahidjo resigned, and was elected without opposition in 1984 and 1988. In 1992, bowing to internal pressure for greater democracy, Biya permitted multiparty elections; although he won, he only received about 40 percent of the vote. In the 1997 election, the first held under the new constitution, Biya received over 92 percent of the vote. The high total occurred because opposition parties boycotted the election, claiming it was unfair. In the October 2004 presidential election, Biya won his second seven-year term with over 70 percent of the vote. Once again, Cameroonian opposition groups claimed the election was rigged.

In 2008, the constitution was amended to allow Biya to run for a third seven-year term as president. He won the October 2011 election with more than 75 percent of the vote.

After the president in importance is the post of prime minister. The prime minister oversees many of the administrative tasks that go along with running a country. Cameroon's prime minister, Philémon Yang, is an Anglophone who was appointed to the office on June 30, 2009.

Philémon Yang, the current prime minister, has held many important positions in Cameroon's government.

LEGISLATIVE BRANCH

The National Assembly is the legislative body of Cameroon's government. It consists of 180 members, who are elected by popular vote to serve five-year terms. The legislature meets for three brief sessions each year: March/April, June/July, and November/December. Legislators can propose and pass laws, but this is relatively rare; instead, they usually vote to approve laws proposed by the president.

Paul Biya has been in power for more than 29 years, making him the longest-serving leader of an African nation. Critics say that he rules as a virtual dictator, and that elections in Cameroon are rigged to keep Biya in power.

According to the 1996 constitution, Cameroon's legislative branch should also include a 100-member Senate. This second legislative body was intended to help decentralize government power. However, the Senate has never been convened. If Cameroon's Senate does ever come into being, one-third of senators are to be presidential appointments, with the remainder chosen by indirect elections. Indirect elections are those in which the people elect delegates who in turn elect officials (much like the Electoral College in the United States).

JUDICIAL BRANCH

As with the legislative branch, the judicial branch of Cameroon's government is subordinate to the executive. The president appoints judges, and the executive branch's Ministry of Justice oversees their performance in court.

The Supreme Court is the top court in Cameroon's judicial system. The Supreme Court establishes the parameters under which lower courts operate, and reviews decisions made at lower levels to determine whether they are in harmony with the constitution and the country's legal code. After the Supreme Court comes the High Court of Justice, a body of nine judges and six substitutes. While Supreme Court judges are appointed by the president, High Court judges are elected by the National Assembly.

Most people's experience with the justice system in Cameroon comes in local courts, which decide issues related to crime, disposition of property, and domestic relations. In different parts of the country, tribal laws and customs are honored when they do not conflict with national laws.

Cameroon's 1996 constitution empowered a Constitution Council to determine whether laws are consistent with the constitution. Like the Senate, however, this regulatory agency has not yet been formed. If it is formed, the president, National Assembly, and Senate will each appoint three people to the Constitution Council.

LOCAL GOVERNMENT

Cameroon is divided into 10 provinces: Littoral, Southwest, West, Northwest, North, Extreme North, East, Centre, Adamawa, and South. Local governments in these provinces are run by councils consisting of a varying number of councilors depending on population.

In 2004 new laws were passed to decentralize the government, giving local lawmakers a broader set of responsibilities. These included control over public utilities (such as water and sewerage facilities or electrical plants), town planning, roads and transportation, community health, civil documentation, education, and leisure.

Remnants of tribal structures persist, however. In the north the predominately Fulani Muslim population still maintains a nomadic lifestyle and embraces a culture that gives local leaders far-reaching powers to make laws,

John Fru Ndi, the leader of the opposition party Social Democratic Front, salutes supporters at a campaign rally.

judge disputes, and detain prisoners. In most cases the state-appointed governors and prefects allow this activity.

POLITICAL PARTIES

Since the early 1990s the government of Cameroon has permitted political parties to form and take part in elections. However, the Cameroon People's Democratic Movement (RPDC) remains the dominant party in Cameroon. The RPDC has maintained control of the national government since Cameroon became independent. The RPDC currently holds 153 seats in the National Assembly.

The main opposition party in Cameroon is the Social Democratic Front (SDF). This party's stated goal is to see Cameroon established as a democracy with free and fair multiparty elections. The SDF has significant support from the Anglophone and Bamileke communities. Its founder and leader is John Fru Ndi. The SDF won 16 Assembly seats in the 2007 elections.

Other political parties in Cameroon include the the National Union for Democracy and Progress (UNDP), which holds 6 seats in the National Assembly; the Democratic Union of Camerron (UDC), which holds 4 seats; and the Progressive Movement (MP) which holds one.

Cameroon's economy depends a great deal on the exploitation of the country's natural resources. (Opposite) Welders work on a pipeline that carries oil from Chad to the port of Kribi in Cameroon. (Right) Enormous logs from the rainforest can be seen in the yard of this sawmill in Douala.

4 A Struggling Economy

FOR TWO DECADES after becoming independent, Cameroon possessed one of Africa's stronger economies, thanks to infrastructure built during the colonial era, its location on the Atlantic, natural resources like oil, and its relative political stability. Today, however, the country is dealing with many of the same problems that other developing countries of sub-Saharan Africa face, including government corruption and a generally unfavorable climate for private businesses. In addition, fluctuations in the international prices of Cameroon's export commodities, such as oil and cocoa, have a significant impact on the economy.

In 2011, the country's *gross domestic product (GDP)*, a measure of the total value of goods and services produced in a year, was $44.3 billion. This ranks 95th of the world's 227 countries.

Based on 2011 data, Cameroon's labor force includes about 7.84 million people. Of that number, 70 percent make their living in agriculture, 13 percent in industry and commerce, and 17 percent in government work or other careers.

INDUSTRY IN CAMEROON

Cameroon is the sixth-largest producer of oil in sub-Saharan Africa. Some of the country's estimated 400 million barrels of oil reserves are located off-shore, while other oil fields are located in coastal areas near Douala and Kribi and in the northern part of the country. Cameroon's oil production has been declining since 2000, as older oil fields are exhausted and fewer new fields are discovered to take their place. However, the country still produces more than 75,000 barrels of oil a day.

The government of Cameroon owns all of the country's oil, and the industry is regulated by the national oil company Societe Nationale des Hydrocarbures (SNH). Foreign oil companies sign agreements with the government, in which they promise to pay a percentage of the profits for the right to develop oil fields.

The United States has invested more than $1 billion in Cameroon's oil sector. This investment is growing, primarily because of the construction of a pipeline that would allow oil from the landlocked country of Chad to be pumped to the Cameroonian port at Kribi. Since it was completed, the 665 mile (1,070 km) pipeline has generated thousands of jobs in both Chad and Cameroon.

Another important natural resource found in Cameroon is bauxite, a mineral that can be refined to make aluminum. Many people are employed

THE ECONOMY OF CAMEROON

Gross domestic product (GDP*):
  $44.33 billion
Inflation: 1.9%
Natural resources: Forests, oil reserves, potential for hydro-electric plants to generate electricity
Agriculture (20% of GDP): coffee, cocoa, cotton, rubber, bananas, oilseed, grains, root starches; livestock; timber
Industry (30.9% of GDP): petroleum production and refining, aluminum production, food processing, light consumer goods, textiles, lumber, ship repair
Services (49.1% of GDP): banking, government, other

Foreign trade:
  Exports–$4.37 billion: crude oil and petroleum products, lumber, cocoa beans, aluminum, coffee, cotton
  Imports–$4.87 billion: machinery, electrical equipment, transport equipment, fuel, food
Economic growth rate: 3%
Currency exchange rate: U.S. $1 = 455.43 Communaute Financiere Africaine (CFA) francs (2011)

*GDP is the total value of goods and services produced in a country annually.
All figures are 2010 estimates unless otherwise indicated.
Source: CIA World Factbook, 2011.

in mining for bauxite, while hundreds of others work at the country's aluminum smelter, which is located in Edea, a city in southern Cameroon. The aluminum smelter is operated as a joint venture between the government and the Canadian firm Alcan.

Processing and packaging of food, especially fruit, is a Cameroonian industry that is growing in importance. Other industries in Cameroon include the manufacture of consumer goods and textiles; the lumber industry, which is actively cutting down the trees of the Mount Cameroon area and the southern high plains; and ship repair facilities in Douala and other ports.

AGRICULTURE IN CAMEROON

Although cash crops like cocoa, coffee, and cotton are grown on large plantations, many people in Cameroon operate small farms and grow just enough food to feed their families. This subsistence farming yields modest quantities of plantains, cocoyams, groundnuts, beans, and other food. In addition, cattle and sheep are raised on farms in some of the northern regions.

Growing numbers of farmers are producing crops for export. These include products like bananas, cotton, soybeans, natural rubber, mangoes, papaya, beef, lamb, pork, fresh and saltwater fish, and rattan. These products are exported from Cameroon to many places around the world.

FOREIGN TRADE

Cameroon's principal customers for its foreign products are European countries, South Korea, and the United States. In 2011, the value of Cameroon's exports was more than $4.3 billion.

Cameroon's principal exports include oil, lumber, aluminum, cocoa, and coffee. Oil remains the country's most valuable natural resource, but Cameroon's cocoa beans are considered among the best in the world. To enhance the cocoa bean crop, the government recently invested $73 million to improve technology and infrastructure, renew aging plant stock, and improve pest control. These measures should help growers gain a solid footing in the world market.

Another important crop is coffee beans, and Cameroonian growers are trying to expand their share of the world market for this commodity. In

A truck loaded with plantains travels past a local market. In recent years Cameroonian farmers have begun exporting plantains, bananas, and other crops to foreign markets.

recent years, an eco-friendly trend has growers developing products that do not damage the rainforest's ecology.

RECESSION AND RECOVERY

From 1960 to 1982, Cameroon's President Ahidjo emphasized a diverse economy and the government invested in health care, education, and infrastructure. As a result, Cameroon was one of the most prosperous African nations for 25 years.

However, a drop in commodity prices for Cameroon's primary exports during the mid-1980s, combined with overvalued currency and economic

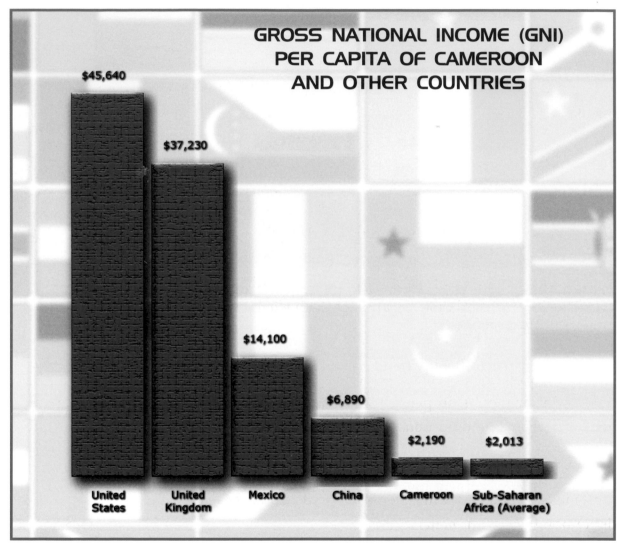

GROSS NATIONAL INCOME (GNI) PER CAPITA OF CAMEROON AND OTHER COUNTRIES

$45,640 — United States
$37,230 — United Kingdom
$14,100 — Mexico
$6,890 — China
$2,190 — Cameroon
$2,013 — Sub-Saharan Africa (Average)

Gross national income per capita is the total value of all goods and services produced domestically in a year, supplemented by income received from abroad, divided by midyear population. The above figures take into account fluctuations in currency exchange rates and differences in inflation rates across global economies, so that an international dollar has the same purchasing power as a U.S. dollar has in the United States.   Source: World Bank, 2011.

mismanagement, led the country into a ten-year *recession*. To turn the economy around, beginning in the late 1980s the government began to implement economic reforms. The salaries of government employees were reduced, some government-controlled industries were turned over to private investors, and the value of the country's currency was adjusted. Cameroon's government also began working with international groups like the World Bank and International Monetary Fund (IMF) to develop its economy, reduce poverty, and improve social services.

By late 2004 Cameroon had met most of its poverty reduction goals, but had not fulfilled all the requirements of the IMF and World Bank. Conversion of government-owned enterprises to private ownership has lagged because of legal and political obstacles, for example. In addition, the government has not nurtured an environment conducive to business. A lack of decent roads and an inefficient rail system keeps products from getting to the port city of Douala on a regular basis. The national airline is underfunded and does not offer regular flights to business centers.

Modernization is desperately needed in transportation, power generation, and telecommunications, but this will not happen any time soon. Cameroon has no investment banks to provide long-term, low-interest loans, so it is hard for *entrepreneurs* to start or build small businesses. These conditions make it difficult for the people to help themselves, leaving them dependent upon the government.

Cameroon is home to hundreds of different ethnic groups. (Opposite) Tribal dancers wearing elaborate costumes perform at a festival. (Right) This group of women is wearing the traditional garb of northwestern Cameroon.

5 A Vibrant Melting Pot of Cultures

CAMEROON'S 250 ETHNIC GROUPS can be divided into eight distinct categories: Cameroon Highlanders (who make up 31 percent of the population); Equatorial Bantu (19 percent); Kirdi (11 percent); Fulani (10 percent); Northwestern Bantu (8 percent); Eastern Nigritic (7 percent); members of other African ethnic groups (13 percent); and non-Africans (less than 1 percent). Twenty-four languages and more than 160 different dialects are spoken in the country, although French is the dominant language used in education, government, commerce, and the media. English is also an important language that is spoken primarily in northwestern Cameroon.

TRADITIONAL LIFE IN NORTHERN AND CENTRAL CAMEROON

The Fulani (also called Fulbe) migrated from the Senegal River Valley into northern Cameroon in the early 19th century. Historically a nomadic people, these Fulani elected to settle into the region and made their living raising livestock and farming. They converted many residents of the region to Islam, often by force.

Pulaaki is the term for the Fulani code of behavior, which sets them apart from other people. It involves complex rules of interaction which focus on self-control, modesty, and respect. Their language, songs, stories, and proverbs reinforce the concept.

Kirdi is a Fulani term used to refer to non-Muslims. This is what the Fulani called other people they encountered during their conquest of northern Cameroon. Those tribes that escaped to the hills, where they could retain their traditional beliefs, cultures, and customs, became known as *kirdi*. Today these people still grow a variety of crops on terraced hill slopes. The largest group is the Matakam, who live in the Mandara Hills.

WESTERN HIGHLANDERS

The Bamileke dominate the western highlands in Cameroon's West Province, where most educated residents speak French. They are divided into approximately 100 smaller groups, ruled by tribal chiefs (called *fons*). They closely identify themselves with their villages rather than their ethnic group. Many are Christian, (particularly Roman Catholic). The most important Bamileke cities and villages include Bafang, Bafoussam, Bandjoun, Bangante, Bawaju, Dschang, and Mbouda.

Bamileke festivals vary from tribe to tribe, but most occur during the dry season to commemorate special events like funerals or the birth of twins. The

THE PEOPLE OF CAMEROON

Population: 19,711,291 (July 2011 est.)*

Ethnic groups: Cameroon Highlanders 31%, Equatorial Bantu 19%, Kirdi 11%, Fulani 10%, Northwestern Bantu 8%, Eastern Nigritic 7%, other African 13%, non-African less than 1%

Age structure:
0–14 years: 40.5%
15–64 years: 56.2%
65 years and over: 3.3%
Birth rate: 33.04/1,000 population
Infant mortality rate: 60.91 deaths/1,000 live births
Death rate: 11.83 deaths/1,000 people
Population growth rate: 2.121%
Life expectancy at birth:
total population: 54.39 years
male: 53.52 years
female: 55.28 years
Total fertility rate: 4.17 children born/woman
Religions: Indigenous beliefs 40%, Christian 40%, Muslim 20%
Languages: 24 major African language groups, English (official), French (official)
Literacy: 67.9% (2001 est.)

*Population estimates for this country explicitly take into account the effects of excess mortality due to AIDS; this can result in lower life expectancy, higher infant mortality and death rates, lower population and growth rates, and changes in the distribution of population by age and sex than would otherwise be expected.

All figures are 2011 estimates unless otherwise indicated.
Source: Adapted from CIA World Factbook, 2011.

Macabo Festival of Bangoua, the Medumba Festival of Bangangté, and the Ben Skin Dance—a dance of female sensuality that has grown increasingly commercialized—are locally celebrated events.

Local art is evident in the *fon*'s court. Specially carved furniture, masks, sculpture, and beading are often used to commemorate the importance of village history during celebrations and special events.

SOUTHERN TROPICAL FOREST GROUP

Thanks to missionary service that predates the German occupation in 1884, the literacy rate among the southern tropical forest people is relatively high. Presbyterianism and Roman Catholicism are the most prevalent Christian denominations, but many people practice their traditional rituals along with Christian ceremonies. While each of the tribal groups have their own languages, most people speak either French or English.

The Pahouin migrated from the savanna region in response to the southward Fulani expansion. There are three important divisions in this ethnic group: Beti, Boulou, and Fang. The Fang are the most numerous of the Pahouin, and are known for their sculptures. They can also be found outside of Cameroon, in countries like Gabon and Equatorial Guinea. The Boulou make up about one-third of the Pahouin peoples, and live primarily in the Dja and Nyong river valleys. The Beti were once hunter-gatherers who now sustain themselves by growing corn, cassava, and cocoa.

INDIGENOUS RELIGION

Religion is a very important part of Cameroon's culture. At least 40 percent of the people practice indigenous beliefs. Although another 40 percent of Cameroonians identify themselves as Christian, many of these people also observe traditional rites and practices. Three indigenous religious groups dominate the country's belief system: the Gbaya, the Nso', and the Bamoun. The Gbaya are found in the southeastern part of Cameroon and spill into the

A traditional healer prepares to perform a religious ritual. More than 40 percent of Cameroon's people still observe traditional religious practices and believe in spirits that can help or harm them.

Central African Republic. The Gbaya believe that supernatural spirits affect the daily lives of believers. They believe that departed ancestors serve as mediators between the spirits and their living relatives. Each person is responsible for his or her own beliefs—there are no priests, rabbis, or imams to point the way.

The Nso' religion is prevalent in the northeast corner of Cameroon's Northwest Province. The Nso' believe in a Supreme Being they call Nyuy. They also believe in the *anyuy*, which are gods and ancestors made divine after they died. They worship their gods through various rituals, though there are two that are particularly important. *Cu*, which honors the ancestors and asks them to intervene on important issues, is a ritual that generally occurs in the middle of March. *Ntanri* is another ritual which honors ancestors.

The Bamoun believe in gods found in nature called *penyinyi*. These are good gods who reward good deeds and punish those who do not obey the laws. There are also evil spirits, the *pagum*, which can live in a person's belly and cause illness or death.

ISLAM AND CHRISTIANITY

The Fulani originally brought Islam to Cameroon. Muslims believe in five important precepts, also known as the Pillars of Islam. The most important of these is the belief in a single god (Allah) and that Muhammad, the founder

Fulani Muslims pray outside a mosque in Cameroon. About 20 percent of Cameroonians follow Islam.

of Islam, was his prophet. Muslims are required to do a number of things, including: pray at different times during each day; give charitable donations to the needy; observe ritual fasting during the holy month of Ramadan; and visit the holy city of Mecca in Saudi Arabia at least once during his or her lifetime, if physically and financially able to do so.

Christianity spread to Cameroon through the work of missionaries, particularly during the 19th and 20th centuries. Today, most Christians in Cameroon are Roman Catholics, Presbyterians, or Baptists. The spread of Christianity significantly affected social, economic, and political life in Cameroon, because the missionaries brought Western customs and culture, as well as languages, education systems, and medicine to the region. In recent years Christian churches have tried to promote peaceful coexistence between the various tribes and population groups in the country, and have protested against government corruption and human rights abuses.

EDUCATION

Cameroon has one of the best educational systems in Africa. The central government provides nursery schools free of charge for children aged four and five. Over 80 percent of the nation's children between the ages of six and 12 attend government-run primary schools. Most of these students live in the southern part of Cameroon. (In the northern provinces, many Muslim children attend religious schools in the evenings. There, they are taught about their religion and memorize passages from the Qur'an, the holy book of Islam.) Secondary school begins at the age of 12 or 13 and lasts for seven years. There are also vocational and technical schools to train students how to be productive farmers. The focus on education has made the adult literacy rate (those age 15 and over who can read and write) in Cameroon 68 percent—one of the highest rates in Africa.

While Cameroon's educational system is highly regarded in Africa, there are areas that need improvement. For example, UNICEF is working in Cameroon to improve educational opportunities for girls. Parents are less likely to send their girls to school if the school is unsanitary, so there has been a focus on cleaning up school facilities. Additionally, UNICEF provides educational materials and trains teachers in order to make schools more welcoming environments for female students.

HEALTH CARE IN CAMEROON

Because of Cameroon's tropical location, diseases such as malaria, cholera, and dysentery are common threats. Other health threats include tuberculosis, sleeping sickness, meningitis, and AIDS. Like many African nations, Cameroon is unable to adequately deal with these diseases because it lacks an effective, modern health care system.

Cameroon has about 250 hospitals, many of which are *subsidized* by the government. However, patients are required to pay for their own health care, and this keeps many Cameroonians from seeking medical help when they need it. Even those who have the money may not be able to make use of the hospital system; 85 percent of Cameroonians do not live near medical facilities, and the lack of good transportation prevents them from getting to hospitals or clinics.

Those who do find their way to a hospital or clinic usually find them overcrowded and understaffed. Even in the best hospitals, sanitation is poor

In recent years the government of Cameroon has tried to educate people about the dangers of HIV/AIDS.

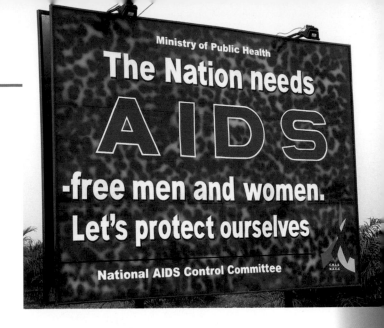

and infection rates relatively high. In addition, doctors and nurses in Cameroon often lack resources that can cure their patients. Drugs that can be used to fight preventable illness are rarely available, so a black market in expired drugs has emerged in many of Cameroon's cities.

Like most African countries, Cameroon faces a great threat from the virus HIV. The virus causes AIDS, a disease that destroys a person's immune system and is almost always fatal if left untreated. According to the World Health Organization, 5.1 percent of sexually active adults (age 15 to 49) in Cameroon are infected with the virus.

In an effort to combat the spread of AIDS, Cameroon has instituted an AIDS education program in its schools with the help of the group Population Services International (PSI). The program stresses *abstinence* for teenagers, while also stressing fidelity and proper condom use among sexually active people, in hopes of reducing infection rates. In addition, the U.S. Embassy in Cameroon has created an HIV Task Force to educate rural community leaders and tribal elders about the dangers of HIV infection.

Cameroon is home to a number of thriving cities. (Opposite) A busy street in downtown Yaoundé, the nation's capital. (Right) Fishing boats on the beach at Limbe, a coastal city in southwest Cameroon.

6 Cities and Communities

Cameroon's cities offer a blend of old and new. Some are modern urban centers complete with high-rise office buildings and the latest conveniences. Others offer hints of cultures past and present.

YAOUNDÉ

Yaoundé is the nation's capital and the regional trade center for coffee, cocoa, sugar cane, and rubber. With a population of 1.4 million, it is Cameroon's second-largest city. As the capital city, it houses government offices, hotels, and the central market, along with foreign embassies, museums, an international airport, and railway lines to Douala and Ngaoundéré. In addition, the presidential palace is located in the Etoudi neighborhood.

Founded in 1888 by a German trader looking for a base for his ivory trade, Yaoundé was occupied by Belgian troops during World War I. During the French mandate period that followed the war, it was the capital of French Cameroon.

The city is known for its markets, with Mokolo being its biggest. The national football team plays often at the Ahmadou Ahidjo (or Ominsport) stadium. Yaoundé is also an educational center with the University of Yaoundé I and II and the Catholic University for Central.

DOUALA

Douala, the capital of the Littoral Province, is named for the ethnic group that first settled the area. With a population of more than 2 million, Douala has the distinction of being Cameroon's largest city and most important port, handling 95 percent of the country's maritime traffic.

Douala's roots trace back to 1472 when, as a small fishing community, its residents were among the first to see the Portuguese explorer Fernando Po step on Cameroonian soil. Early on Douala was a trading port that served as a key connection in the West African slave trade. The city came under German control in 1884 and French control in 1919.

Today, Douala is a major center of trade for the Central African Republic, Chad, Equatorial Guinea, and the Republic of Congo. Exporters and importers have multiple transportation options: an international airport, a railway station, and modern roads for trucks and cars. As the nation's economic hub, Douala handles most of the country's exports. People there are involved in the manufacture, processing, and distribution of oil, cocoa, coffee, aluminum products, beer, soft drinks, textiles, and timber. The city has four distinct neighborhoods named after the original ruling families: Akwa,

Pedestrians walk through a street in Douala, the nation's largest city.

the commercial district; Bonapriso, the upscale residential quarter; Bananjo, the administrative section; and Bonaberi, the industrial area.

LIMBE

In the Southwest Province lies Limbe, a small resort town with a population of about 85,000. Located at the foot of Mount Cameroon, about 46 miles (74 km) from Douala, Limbe is known for its gorgeous black sand beaches.

Limbe was founded by the Baptist Missionary Society of London and it was known as Victoria until 1982. Baptist missionary Alfred Saker purchased the land from King William of Bimbia to establish a base for his work. Cocoa, palm, rubber, and banana plantations grew and expanded around Victoria after World War II.

Economically speaking, the town's commerce centers around weekend vacationers and urbanites who want to spend time at the Ambas Bay beaches. In addition to its inviting coastline, traditional dances, music, and wrestling tournaments draw visitors from nearby coastal villages.

BAMENDA

Considered the cradle of political pluralism of Cameroon, Bamenda is the capital of the Northwest Province. Its residents have been the heart of the Social Democratic Front (SDF), the English-speaking opposition movement against French-speaking dominance. It is a metropolis with a population of nearly 400,000 located 227 miles (365 km) northwest of Yaoundé.

Bamenda, also known as Abakwa, is a city with many markets, banks, offices, and coffee processing facilities. Local baskets, beads, woodcarvings, and bronze statues are available for tourists. Visitors will also find culture sites to explore, such as the Mankon Fon's Palace, a cultural history museum, and the Bali Fon's Palace.

KUMBO

Also located in the Northwest Province, Kumbo is one of the area's largest towns; it has a population of over 116,000 people. Part of the Nso' linguistic group, the Banso people, live there. They are known for hosting a famous horseracing festival every November that features both Fulani and Banso equestrians.

Kumbo has a rather large market with one section devoted to traditional medicine. Two of Cameroon's better hospitals are also located in Kumbo: Banso Baptist Hospital in Kumbo, and Shisong Catholic Hospital, located just outside of town.

GAROUA

Throughout the 1800s Garoua was part of the African Muslim state of Sokoto. On November 1, 1901, German colonial forces took over the town; the Germans were replaced by French rulers in June 1915. Garoua remained under French control until the independence of Cameroon in 1960.

A city of nearly 500,000 people, Garoua is Cameroon's third-busiest port and the hub of its region's commercial development. The city serves as a crossroads for goods from Cameroon, Chad, and Nigeria. A textile processing plant and an airport grace the birth city of the nation's first president, Ahmadou Ahidjo. It is a modern city with tall buildings, banks, markets, industry, and an international airport.

Garoua is about 400 miles (643 km) northwest of Yaoundé. It has a port on the Bénoué River, a broad tributary of the Niger. The region is dominated by the Fulani, and is an important Fulani political center.

A CALENDAR OF CAMEROONIAN FESTIVALS

Muslim Holidays

The dates of Muslim holidays, such as **Ramadan**, are determined using a lunar calendar that is shorter than the 365-day solar year used in Western countries. This means that each year, Muslim holidays are held 10 or 11 days earlier than the year before. Thus, any Muslim holiday could be celebrated during any month in the Western calendar.

The **Muslim New Year** marks the beginning of the Islamic month known as Muharram.

Mawlid an-Nabi, the commemoration of the birthday of the Prophet Muhammad, is celebrated by prayer and often a procession to the local mosque. Families gather for feasts, often featuring the foods that were reportedly the favorites of Mohammed: dates, grapes, almonds, and honey. This holiday occurs on the 12th day of the month Rabi'-ul-Awwal.

The month of **Ramadan** is a perhaps the best-known Islamic calendar event. During Ramadan, Muslims are supposed to fast during the day, pray, and perform deeds of kindness for the poor. At the end of Ramadan comes **Eid al-Fitr**, a feast and celebration lasting three days. During Eid al-Fitr, schools and businesses close, and people put on new clothing and exchange presents.

Eid al-Adha is celebrated on the 10th day of the Islamic month of Dhul Hijja. It observes the Prophet Ibrahim's (Abraham's) willingness to sacrifice his son for God.

January

On January 1 the country celebrates its independence, which came by UN decree in 1960.

Nyem-Nyem is the annual festival in the Adamawa centered around Ngaoundéré; it celebrates the heroic resistance of the people against German occupation. Traditional festivities are held around caves on the top of Mount Djim.

The **Mount Cameroon Race** is a grueling 17-mile (27 km) race up and down the 9,843-foot (3,000-m) mountain.

February

February 11 is **Youth Day**.

May

Commemoration of **National Institutions Day** celebrates the first meeting in 1957 of Cameroon's Legislative Assembly.

May 20 is **Constitution Day**, commemorating the ratification of Cameroon's constitution of 1972.

July

The **Medumba Festival** in Bangangte is held every two years, normally in July. This festival promotes the Medumba language and the artwork of the 13 local villages.

A CALENDAR OF CAMEROONIAN FESTIVALS

October

October 1 celebrates **Unification Day**, observing the unification of French and British Cameroon. The Southern region voted to merge with Cameroon in 1961 while the Northern region aligned with Nigeria.

December

Ngondo Festival of the Sawa is the first week of December for the coast dwellers of Cameroon from Limbe to Kribi. This festival focuses on the Wouri River. The ritual and feast celebrates the unity of the Sawa peoples and their ancestors who they believe live in the water. Traditional dances, choral music, crafts, a canoe parade and race, a carnival, and a diver collecting ancestors' messages from the bottom of the river are some of the day's events.

December 10 is **Human Rights Day**, started in 1948 to celebrate the United Nations' Universal Declaration of Human Rights.

RECIPES

West African Chicken-Peanut Soup

Makes 12 servings

4 tbs. Oriental (dark) sesame oil
2 cups diced cooked chicken breast
1 cup chopped onions
1 tbs. minced garlic
1 tbs. curry powder
1 tsp. salt
1 tsp. black pepper
1/2 to 1 tsp crushed red pepper flakes
6 cups canned or homemade chicken broth
1/2 cup tomato paste
1 15-oz. can chopped stewed tomatoes
1/4 cup plus 2 tbs. chunky peanut butter

Directions:
1. In large skillet, over medium heat, heat the sesame oil. Add chicken, onion, and garlic and sauté over medium heat until onion is translucent.
2. Add curry powder, salt, pepper, red pepper flakes, chicken broth, tomato paste, stewed tomatoes and peanut butter. Heat thoroughly, but don't boil. Serve hot.

Sese Plantains

Serves 2

2 large green plantains
10 1/2 cups water
2 medium tomatoes, peeled and chopped
hot pepper, to taste
1 large onion, peeled and chopped
1/2 cube vegetable stock (optional)
1 tbs. palm oil
salt, to taste
roasted cashew nuts, to garnish

Directions:
1. Peel and cut each plantain into 6 rounds. Put into a saucepan with water and boil for 10 minutes. Add the tomatoes, pepper, and onion and cook for another 10 minutes. Crumble in the vegetable stock cube. Cover the saucepan and let it simmer on medium for at least 5 minutes, before stirring the oil into the food.
2. Let it cook for another 10 minutes and season to taste. Sprinkle with roasted cashew nuts to serve. The salt should only be put in when the plantains are cooked.

Zom (Spinach with meat)

Serves 6-8

2 pounds stew beef, cut into small cubes
water
4 tbs. oil
1 large onion, chopped
2 pounds spinach, washed and chopped
2 tomatoes chopped finely
1 tbs. tomato paste
2 tbs. peanut butter
salt and pepper

Directions:
1. Put the beef in saucepan with a little salt and enough water to cover. Bring to a boil, cover, and simmer for 1 1/2 to 2 hours until the meat is just tender. The time will vary depending on the cut of meat and the size of the pieces. Remove the meat and keep the liquid.
2. Using a large pan, heat the oil and sauté the onion until soft. Add meat pieces and cook for two minutes.
3. Take 2 cups of the reserved beef broth. Add water if necessary, then pour this in pan with onion and meat. Add spinach, tomatoes, tomato paste, peanut butter, pepper and salt. Bring to a boil and then cover, reduce heat and simmer for 30 minutes, stirring regularly. Serve with rice.

Banana Bread

1 3/4 cups flour
1 cup sugar
1 tsp. baking soda
2 eggs, beaten
1 tsp. baking powder
3 medium ripe bananas mashed
2 tbs. margarine
salt

Directions:

1. Preheat oven to 350°F (177°C). Grease and flour one loaf pan. In a bowl, sift the flour together with baking soda, baking powder, and a little salt.
2. In a larger bowl, cream the margarine and sugar. Then add the beaten eggs a little at a time. Add flour alternately with mashed bananas; stir well to mix ingredients but do not over-stir.
3. Put mixture into prepared loaf pan. Bake for approximately one hour or until toothpick inserted in middle comes out clean. Remove from oven and cool in pan for 15 minutes. Turn out on wire rack to finish cooling.

Fried Sweet Potatoes or Plantains

3-4 plantains or 4 medium sweet potatoes, well scrubbed
Oil (peanut, soybean, or safflower)

Directions:

1. Use either peanut, soybean, or safflower oil to deep-fry, as they have a high smoking temperature. If you have a cooking thermometer, keep the oil around 350°F (177°C). Heat the oil in a heavy saucepan.
2. Slice the sweet potatoes or peeled plantains into 1/4-inch rounds. Fry the slices a few at a time until they are golden and crisp on the outside but still soft on the inside. If fried too long, the inside will toughen,

so try a couple to get the best timing. Remove them from the oil with a slotted spoon and drain on paper towels or newspaper.
3. Usually fried sweet potatoes and plantains are just sprinkled with salt and hot sauce (Tabasco works!), but sometimes they are coated with powdered ginger and/or cayenne before frying and then salted. If you prefer a sweet taste, sprinkle with sugar and cinnamon.

Cameroon Suya

Serves 4
1 lb. round or flank steak
1/2 tsp. sugar
1 tsp. garlic powder
1 tsp. ground ginger
1 tsp. paprika
1 tsp. ground cinnamon
pinch of chili powder
2 tsp. onion salt
1/2 cup peanuts, finely crushed
vegetable oil, for brushing

Directions:

1. Trim the steak of fat and then cut into 1-inch wide strips. Place in a bowl or a shallow dish. Mix the sugar, garlic powder, spices and onion salt together in a small bowl. Add the crushed peanuts, then add this mixture to the steak, mixing well so that the spices are worked into the meat.
2. Thread the steak on to six satay sticks, pushing the meat close together. Place satays in a shallow dish, cover loosely with foil, and marinate in a cool place for a few hours.
3. Preheat a broiler or barbecue grill. Brush the meat with a little oil and then cook over a moderate heat for about 15 minutes, until evenly brown.

GLOSSARY

abstinence—to deliberately refrain from sexual intercourse.

annex—the incorporation of territory into an existing political entity, such as a state or a city.

commodity—an article of trade or commerce, especially an agricultural or mining product that can be processed and resold.

coup—the sudden violent overthrow of an existing government.

entrepreneur—a person who initiates, operates, and assumes the risk of growing a business or enterprise.

estuary—a place where the sea extends inland to meet the mouth of a river.

exchange economy—an economy that operates by voluntary exchange in a free market and is not planned or controlled by a central authority; an economic system based on capitalist principles.

federation—an encompassing political or societal entity formed by uniting smaller or more localized entities.

fertile—capable of sustaining abundant plant growth.

feudal—a political, economic, or social order that is based on the ruling body owning land while the workers (or vassals) work the land for a profit. The workers are duty-bound to pay homage to the landowners and to enter into military service upon command of the landowner.

gross domestic product (GDP)—the total value of the goods and services produced by the residents of a nation during a specified period (usually a year).

indigenous—having originated in and being produced, growing, living, or occurring naturally in a particular region or environment.

infrastructure—the basic facilities and services needed for a community to function, like water, sewer, and power lines, roads, schools, post offices, and prisons.

limnic eruption—a rare natural occurrence in which a cloud of carbon dioxide gas is unexpectedly released from a body of water.

mandate—a commission granted by the League of Nations to a member nation for the establishment of a responsible government over a particular territory.

marginalize—to force to the extreme edge of a social group.

monopoly—a situation in which a company or group has exclusive control over a commercial activity.

nomadic—having no set place to live. Nomads move from place to place, usually within a defined region or territory.

plateau—a rather large, level expanse normally found on a mountain, a large hill, or an elevated region.

plebiscite—a vote by which members of a community express their will on an important question.

recession—a period of reduced economic activity.

savanna—a treeless, grassy plain in a tropical or subtropical region.

subsidy—public money used to assist or promote a particular group, such as farmers or to keep prices stable in an industry, such as health care.

terrace—a planting method that supports vegetation on a raised bank of earth having a vertical or sloping sides and a flat top.

Monopolize Cameroon

Adapt the game of Monopoly to the Cameroon expansion. Divide your class into two teams, each representing a European country (perhaps Germany and Great Britain) whose goal is to exploit the country's resources. Two of the players from each team will remain by the board to play out the game. The rest of the class will be located on far sides of the room. They will represent Parliament and European business interests and have money at their disposal. The two players at the board will play the game. One will control the board while the other serves as a runner who will communicate with people in their home offices and parliament. The object of the game will be to acquire as much property and/or as many hotels as possible during their time of play. The players will communicate their needs to parliament throughout the game, but may have to make decisions before the runner returns. If parliament is unhappy with the players' decision, they can elect to have the player replaced and send in someone else from their team. The game can end after the players round the board once or twice. Afterwards, discuss what you've learned through the process.

Create a poster for endangered animals

Find photos on the Internet or in magazines of endangered species in Cameroon. Write a paragraph or two about what type of habitat they need and why they are important. Take this a step further and design posters pleading the case for these endangered species and why they should be saved. Approach your local newspaper and see if they will publicize the poster, perhaps in conjunction with an eco-group.

Map

Make a salt map of Cameroon with different colors for difference provinces. Try to duplicate or represent the topography as well. (For recipes to mix the ingredients for the salt map, try this Web site: http://www.cooks.com/rec/search/0,1-0,salt_maps,FF.html.)

Historically Speaking (or, "You Were There")

Write and produce a short play about significant moments in Cameroon's history, like Fernando Po's arrival to Cameroon, the negotiations for the city of Victoria, or the beginning of the German occupation.

Report Ideas

Using an encyclopedia or other reference books, present the pros or cons for harvesting the rain forest. Use visual aids. You could team up with another student who will present the opposing view.

Cameroon has several active volcanoes. Develop a report and/or develop a demonstration about what happens when volcanoes erupt. Chart eruptions in the past. Is there a trend? A pattern? Do you think there will be eruptions in the future? Why or why not? Justify your answer.

The Chad-Cameroon pipeline is a bit controversial. Report on the pros and cons. Why should it be completed and why not? Who will it help? Consider developing a model of the pipeline network.

Create a wildlife refuge

Using photos downloaded from the Internet and drawings, adopt an animal from Cameroon. Do some specific research about the animal: where it lives, how it lives, what it eats, how much room it needs to grow. Note what animals prey upon this animal and how it protects itself. You could make masks to depict the animal you have researched. If your entire class participates, invite faculty and parents or other students to come into your classroom's "wildlife preserve" where the guests can actually talk to the "animals" and find out how they live.

CHRONOLOGY

1472:   Portuguese seafarer Fernando Po arrives at the Bight of Biafra and sails into the estuary of what is now called the Wouri River in Cameroon.

1520:   The Portuguese establish sugar plantations on the islands of São Tomé and Bioko (formerly called Fernando Po). The slave trade flourishes.

1807:   Britain outlaws its own slave trade and tries to abolish the trade in humans along the Gulf of Guinea.

1845:   Baptists missionaries start the first English settlement in Cameroon, near Douala on the Cameroon River.

1858:   Alfred Saker buys land from King William of Bimbia and builds a permanent settlement, which he names Victoria, at the foot of Mount Cameroon.

1860:   Woermann and Company (Hamburg merchants and traders) establish the first German trade factory in the estuary on the coast.

1884:   German leaders sign agreements with multiple kings to establish trade and occupy the territory.

1886:   Germans buy English missionaries' holdings in Victoria.

1914:   Germany invades Belgium in August, beginning World War I.

1922:   The League of Nations puts Cameroon under British and French administration after Germans lose in World War I.

1946:   The United Nations declares Cameroon a trust territory, with France and Britain continuing to rule their respective areas.

1960:   French Cameroon gains independence as the Republic of Cameroon. Ahmadou Ahidjo is elected president.

1961:   In a plebiscite, the southern part of British Cameroon votes to unite with French Cameroon, while the northern region elects to join Nigeria.

1966:   President Ahidjo makes Cameroon a one-party state.

1972:   The Federal Republic of Cameroon is renamed the United Republic of Cameroon when a new constitution is written.

1980: Ahidjo is reelected president for a fifth five-year term.

1982: Ahidjo resigns and names Paul Biya as the next president.

1984: Biya is elected president and abolishes the office of prime minister.

1988: Biya is reelected as president.

1990: The National Assembly adopts legislation officially declaring Cameroon a multiparty state.

1991: About 300 people are killed throughout Cameroon in pro-democracy demonstrations, large-scale strikes, and other actions to force institutional reforms.

1992: Presidential election is conducted. Opposition parties, and international observers accuse Biya of electoral fraud and other irregularities.

1999: UN Human Rights Committee criticizes Cameroon for its alleged failure to protect and respect fundamental human rights.

2000: Construction of the Chad-Cameroon oil pipeline begins.

2004: Paul Biya is elected to a third term as president on October 11.

2007: SDF leader John Fru Ndi asks for legislative and municipal elections to be postponed until a voter registration drive has been completed.

2008: National Assembly amends constitution to allow Biya to run for a third term and grants him immunity from legal prosecution; Nigeria relinquishes control of Bakassi peninsula to Cameroon after a long-standing dispute.

2010: Senior security officials are fired following rumors of a failed military coup.

2011: Biya is re-elected president for a third term with over 75 percent of the vote.

2012: Despite intervention by Cameroon's military, hundreds of elephants are killed by poachers in Bouba Ndjida National Park.

FURTHER READING/INTERNET RESOURCES

Ignatowski, Clare A. *Journey of Song: Public Life and Morality in Cameroon*. Indiana University Press, 2006.

Kummer, Patricia K. *Cameroon* (Enchantment of the World). Children's Press, 2004

Mbaku, John Mukum. *Culture and Customs of Cameroon*. Greenwood Press, 2005.

Sheehan, Sean. *Cameroon* (Cultures of the World). Benchmark Books, 2011.

West, Ben. *Cameroon: The Bradt Travel Guide*, 2nd Edition. Guilford, Conn.: The Globe Pequot Press, 2008.

Travel Information

http://www.lonelyplanet.com/cameroon
http://travel.state.gov/travel/cis_pa_tw/cis/cis_1081.html
http://www.world66.com/africa/cameroon

History and Geography

http://www.africa.com/cameroon
http://africanhistory.about.com/od/cameroon/Cameroon.htm
http://www.factmonster.com/ipka/A0107382.html

Economic and Political Information

http://news.bbc.co.uk/2/hi/africa/country_profiles/1042937.stm
http://www.ambacam-usa.org/
http://www.spm.gov.cm/index_ac.php?lang=en

Culture and Festivals

http://www.ethnologue.com/show_country.asp?name=Cameroon
http://www.everyculture.com/Bo-Co/Cameroon.html
http://travel.mapsofworld.com/cameroon/festivals-and-events.html

FOR MORE INFORMATION

Embassy of the Republic of Cameroon
1700 Wisconsin Ave. N.W.,
Washington, DC 20007
Tel: (202) 265-8790
Fax: (202) 387-3826
Email: mail@cameroonembassyusa.org
Website: http://www.ambacam-usa.org/embassy.aspx

United States Embassy in Cameroon
Avenue Rosa Parks
P.O. Box 817,
Yaounde, Cameroon
Tel: (237) 220-15-00
Fax: (237) 220-15-00 ext. 4531
Website: http://cameroon.usembassy.gov

Tourism Authority
B.P. 266,
Yaounde, 237
Cameroon
Tel: (237) 222-4411
Fax: (237) 222-1295
Website: www.cameroontourist.com

U.S. Department of State
Bureau of Consular Affairs
2100 Pennsylvania Ave. NW, 4th Floor
Washington, DC 20037
Tel: (202) 736 9130

INDEX

Numbers in **bold italic** refer to captions.

CONTRIBUTORS/PICTURE CREDITS

Professor Robert I. Rotberg is Director of the Program on Intrastate Conflict and Conflict Resolution at the Kennedy School, Harvard University, and President of the World Peace Foundation. He is the author of a number of books and articles on Africa, including *A Political History of Tropical Africa* and *Ending Autocracy, Enabling Democracy: The Tribulations of Southern Africa*.

Diane Cook is an award-winning journalist and freelance writer, as well as a speaker and international traveler. She has received the Associated Press Chesapeake's Mark Twain Award, various MDDC Press Association awards, and an honorable mention from the Freedom Foundation. Diane also wrote *Pathfinders of the American Frontier* (Mason Crest, 2002). She lives in Dover, Delaware, with her husband David.